ANIMALS
Communicate

by Nadia Ali

PEBBLE
a capstone imprint

Published by Pebble, an imprint of Capstone
1710 Roe Crest Drive, North Mankato, Minnesota 56003
capstonepub.com

Library of Congress Cataloging-in-Publication Data is available on the Library of Congress website.

ISBN: 9780756571764 (hardcover)
ISBN: 9780756571719 (paperback)
ISBN: 9780756571726 (ebook PDF)

Summary: Whales whistle, fireflies glow, and skunks spray—that's how they communicate! Find out how mammals, reptiles, birds, and other animals send messages and signals to stay safe, make friends, and care for their young.

Editorial Credits:
Editor: Kristen Mohn; Designer: Tracy Davies; Media Researcher: Svetlana Zhurkin; Production Specialist: Katy LaVigne

Image Credits:
Alamy: Nature Picture Library, 19; Getty Images: Ali Majdfar, 26, Alphotographic, 29, ArgenLant, 5, Magnus Larsson, 25, Marc Guitard, 24, Paul Starosta, 27, Romona Robbins Photography, 6, Tom Brakefield, 16; Shutterstock: Alan Jeffery, 18, Artush, 8, Asian Images, 13, Charles T. Peden, 11, cornfield, 1, 20, Coulanges, 17, Foto Mous, 9, Jason Patrick Ross, 15, JayPierstorff, 7, Mike Dexter, 21, Reimar, 12, Sourabh Bharti, 23, Stephan Hawks, 22, teekayu, 10, Tomas Kotou, 14, Tory Kallman, 28, Warren Metcalf, cover

Printed and bound in China 5132

TABLE OF CONTENTS

Words in **bold** are in the glossary.

How Do Animals Communicate?

People smile, wave, hug, and talk to communicate. Animals don't use words, but they communicate too! They send signals through sound, smell, touch, and **body language** that can be seen.

Look outside. Ants march. Bees dance. Fireflies glow. They are busy communicating!

Sound

Whales swim in **pods**. They click, whistle, and squeak to each other. The clicks help them find their way. The whistles and squeaks keep the group together.

Coyotes howl. It can mean "Where are you?" Or it can mean "Danger!" A howl can be heard up to 3 miles (4.8 kilometers) away. Coyotes howl so much that they are called singing dogs.

Geckos are called chatty lizards.
They communicate through squeaks,
clicks, and chirps. Different chirps can
mean "Keep away!" or "I like you!"

Do you hum when you eat? Gorillas do. If something is tasty, they make a low hum. When they eat their favorite food, they sing!

Every gorilla has its own song. They could be saying "Yummy!" or "Have you tried this?"

Porcupines are covered in spikes. But they need more ways to scare off **predators**. They chatter their teeth to say "Go away!" They also grunt, groan, and screech to communicate with other porcupines.

Rabbits are very, very quiet. They mostly communicate with body language. They stand up straight and tall. They thump their back legs. These actions mean they are scared, worried, or angry.

Scent

People send notes and emails. Bears leave messages with scent!

Bears stand and rub their backs on tree trunks. The more trees they rub, the more messages they send to other bears. These messages help bears find the right **mate**.

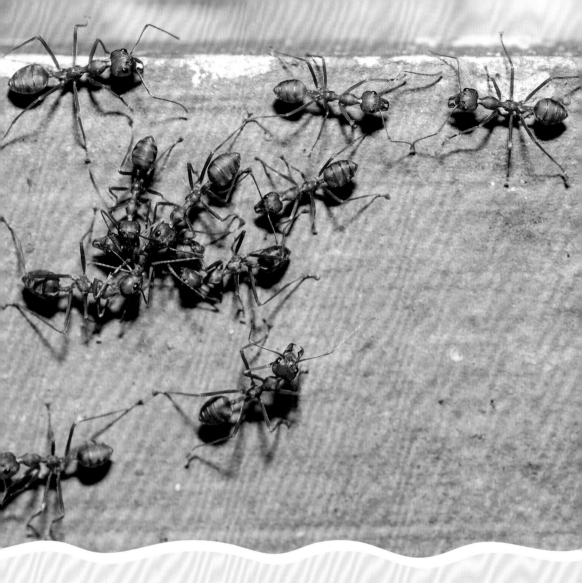

Ants leave a scent on their trail. The scent leads other ants from the nest to food. Each ant adds to the scent as it follows the trail.

Great white sharks have a good sense of smell. They can smell a drop of blood in the water from a quarter mile away. The scent leads them to food.

A shark only smells with its **nostrils**. It breathes through its **gills**.

Snakes have nostrils, but they mostly smell with their tongues. A snake has a special organ in its mouth. It is called the **Jacobson's organ**. When it flicks its tongue in the air, the organ tells the snake what the scent is. The scents give the snake information.

Skunks thump and grunt to send messages. They also use scent to stay safe. Skunks spray predators with a strong scent called **musk**. It says "Keep away!"

Male lions guard their area with pee! Their pee leaves a scent behind. It tells others "This is mine!" Lions also roar and chase to let strangers know they are not welcome.

Touch

Did you know that chimpanzees comb their hair? Chimps **groom** each other to pick out bugs and dirt. It helps build trust.

Grooming is a way to show who is in charge. The chimp with the lower **rank** does the grooming.

When the weather is very cold, emperor penguins huddle together for warmth. They take turns standing in the middle. It is the warmest spot! One penguin moves to let the others know it's time to switch places.

Humans use their arms to hug. Have you ever seen horses hug? A horse rests its head or neck on another horse. Hugging is one way horses show care for each other.

Not all touch between animals is friendly. Male giraffes swing their long necks against each other. Getting hit can hurt! They fight to decide who is the best giraffe.

An elephant uses its trunk to hold things, to make sounds, and to eat. It also uses its trunk to show friendship. An elephant may wrap its trunk around another elephant's trunk. This means "I'm here for you."

Tigers are like big cats when it comes to touch. A mother rubs her face against her cubs. This tells the cubs they are cared for. It also puts her scent on the cubs so they can find each other.

Sight

People smile when they're happy. Monkeys can share feelings with their faces too. But not every monkey smile is friendly. A smile with clenched teeth and curled lips means "I am ready to bite!"

Octopuses are experts at **camouflage**. It is how they communicate and defend themselves. They change color to shock predators. If they are scared, they might turn white. "Boo!"

Fireflies use light to send messages to each other. Each firefly has its own light pattern. They use light to say different things. A slow glow can mean "Let's hang out!"

When bees find **pollen**, they return to the **hive** dancing! It is called a waggle dance. It shows other bees how to get to the flowers. Then the other bees can help collect the pollen.

Dolphins leap out of the water to communicate. A leap may tell others "Shark below!" or "I am the leader." A leaping mother may be saying "Come back here!" to her baby.

Many people think peacocks are beautiful. Peacocks think so too!

The male peacock spreads his tail feathers like a fan. This gets the attention of female peacocks. Colorful feathers say "Hey, look at me!"

Glossary

body language (BAHD-ee LANG-gwij)—movements animals make to communicate with each other

camouflage (CAM-uh-flazh)—patterns or colors on an animal's skin that help it hide

gill (GIL)—a body part used to breathe underwater

groom (GROOM)—to keep clean; apes and monkeys groom each other by picking bugs off each other's fur

hive (HIVE)—a place where a group of bees lives

Jacobson's organ (JAY-kub-sons OR-gun)—an organ on the roof of the mouth of a reptile; the tongue picks up scents and carries them to the Jacobson's organ

mate (MAYT)—one of a pair that join together to produce young

musk (MUSSK)—an oil that some animals produce

nostril (NAH-stril)—an opening in the nose used to breathe or smell

pod (PODD)—a group of whales

pollen (PAW-len)—a powder made by flowers to help them create new seeds

predator (PREH-duh-tur)—an animal that hunts other animals for food

rank (RANK)—a place in the social order

Read More

Combs, Carolyn. *What's This Tail Saying?* Nevada City, CA: Dawn Publications, 2020.

Hodgkins, Fran. *Thump Goes the Rabbit: How Animals Communicate.* New York: HarperCollins, 2020.

Raatma, Lucia. *A Colony of Bees.* North Mankato, MN: Capstone, 2020.

Internet Sites

Britannica Kids: Animal Communication
kids.britannica.com/students/article/animal-communication/272879

PBS: Nature: Emperor Penguins Huddle to Keep Warm
pbs.org/video/nature-emperor-penguins-huddle-keep-warm

Wonderopolis: How Do Animals Communicate?
wonderopolis.org/wonder/how-do-animals-communicate

Index

About the Author

Nadia Ali is a children's book author. She writes in various genres and is especially fond of animals. Inspired by her kitty, Cici, she contributes pet articles and features to magazines and websites. Nadia was born in London and currently resides in the Caribbean, where she happily swapped out London's gray skies for clear blue skies. She lives with her husband and has two married daughters.